The Kopi Luwak Legacy: Tradition, Taste and Truth

THE KOPI LUWAK LEGACY: TRADITION, TASTE AND TRUTH

First edition. December 22, 2024.

ISBN: 979-8230977858

Written by Dans Hardyans.

Table of Contents

Introduction

Kopi Luwak, often referred to as the most exotic and expensive coffee in the world, is more than just a beverage—it's a story of nature, tradition, and human ingenuity. Originating from the lush coffee plantations of Southeast Asia, this rare brew owes its uniqueness to an unexpected ally in the animal kingdom: the civet, or luwak, whose role in the coffee production process has fascinated connoisseurs and casual drinkers alike.

This book takes you on a journey to uncover the legacy of Kopi Luwak, from its humble beginnings in the forests of Indonesia to its recognition as a global luxury. Along the way, we'll explore the cultural traditions and rich heritage surrounding this coffee, its meticulous production process, and the ongoing debates about sustainability and ethics in its industry.

Kopi Luwak is not merely a coffee; it is an experience that encapsulates the harmonious blend of nature's artistry and human craftsmanship. As you delve into these pages, you'll gain a deeper appreciation for the intricate journey that transforms a simple coffee bean into a sip of unparalleled elegance.

This book invites you to savor the story behind the brew, to explore its roots, and to reflect on the complexities of its production. Whether you are a coffee enthusiast or a curious reader, the world of Kopi Luwak holds surprises and insights that will leave you captivated.

Let us embark on this flavorful journey together.

Chapter 1: The Arrival of Coffee in Southeast Asia

The story of coffee begins centuries ago in the ancient lands of Ethiopia, where the discovery of the energizing properties of coffee beans gave rise to one of the most popular beverages in human history. From there, coffee traveled across continents, eventually reaching the vibrant and fertile lands of Southeast Asia, particularly Indonesia.

The Dutch and the Introduction of Coffee to Indonesia

In the 17th century, the Dutch East India Company played a pivotal role in introducing coffee to Indonesia, specifically to the islands of Java, Sumatra, and Sulawesi. Recognizing the archipelago's ideal climate and volcanic soil, the Dutch established large-scale coffee plantations that quickly flourished. Coffee became a vital commodity in global trade, and Indonesia soon emerged as one of the largest producers of coffee in the world.

These plantations were primarily cultivated by local farmers under the colonial system, which often subjected them to harsh labor conditions. Despite this, the local population developed a deep connection with coffee, incorporating it into their daily lives and rituals.

Coffee's Cultural Roots in Southeast Asia

As coffee spread across Southeast Asia, it became more than just a trade item—it became a cultural staple. In Indonesia, for example, coffee is deeply woven into social gatherings, family traditions, and local ceremonies. Traditional coffee houses, known as warungs kopi, became popular meeting places where people of all walks of life would gather to share stories and enjoy the rich aroma of freshly brewed coffee.

The Unique Evolution of Indonesian Coffee

Indonesia's geographical diversity contributed to the creation of distinct coffee profiles, with each island producing beans that reflected its unique terroir. Java coffee, for instance, is known for its full-bodied, earthy flavor, while Sumatran coffee is admired for its complex, herbaceous notes. These regional varieties laid the foundation for Indonesia's reputation as a haven for coffee lovers.

The Birth of Kopi Luwak

Amid this rich history of coffee cultivation, an extraordinary discovery was made during the early 18th century. Local farmers noticed that the Asian palm civet, or luwak, had a peculiar preference for ripe coffee cherries. These animals would eat the cherries, and their digestive process would alter the beans inside, resulting in a unique flavor profile. This accidental discovery would later give birth to Kopi Luwak, a coffee unlike any other.

This chapter sets the stage for understanding how coffee, particularly Kopi Luwak, became an integral part of Southeast Asia's identity and a symbol of Indonesia's contribution to the world of coffee. As we delve deeper into the next chapters, we'll uncover the fascinating processes, traditions, and stories that make Kopi Luwak an enduring legacy.

—

Chapter 2: Kopi Luwak – From Nature to Cup

Kopi Luwak, celebrated for its rarity and exceptional flavor, stands as a testament to the fascinating interplay between nature and human ingenuity. Its journey, unlike any other coffee, begins not in the hands of farmers but with the Asian palm civet, a small, nocturnal mammal native to Southeast Asia.

The Unique Role of the Civet

The process of creating Kopi Luwak starts with the civet's discerning palate. These animals are selective in their eating habits, naturally choosing only the ripest and sweetest coffee cherries from the coffee trees in their natural habitat. The civet consumes these cherries as part of its diet, and the beans inside the cherries pass through its digestive system.

During this process, the cherries undergo fermentation inside the civet's stomach. This fermentation process, caused by enzymes in the digestive tract, alters the beans chemically. The beans lose some of their natural bitterness and acidity, resulting in a smoother, more rounded flavor profile once roasted. The civet's natural selection of cherries and the fermentation process play crucial roles in giving Kopi Luwak its unique taste.

After the beans pass through the civet's digestive system, they are excreted in their whole form, still encased in their parchment layer. While this might sound unappealing, it is precisely this journey through the civet's digestive tract that imparts the coffee beans with their signature smoothness, reduced acidity, and complex flavor.

Harvesting the Beans

Farmers and coffee collectors venture into the forest or collect droppings from designated civet enclosures. This step requires a great deal of care and expertise to ensure that only the highest-quality beans are selected for further processing. The beans are carefully sorted to remove any debris and impurities, as only the best beans are suitable for the coffee-making process.

This part of the process is both labor-intensive and delicate, requiring skill and attention to detail to ensure that the coffee's quality is preserved from the very beginning. The collected beans are then brought to a facility for further cleaning and processing.

Washing and Cleaning

Once collected, the beans must undergo an intensive cleaning process. The beans are thoroughly washed in freshwater to remove any residual materials, including any remnants from the civet's digestive tract. This ensures the beans are sanitized without compromising their unique flavor. Farmers typically clean the beans by hand, ensuring that no detail is overlooked.

The cleaning process is crucial, as any contaminants left on the beans can negatively affect the taste. This multi-step cleaning process is done with great care, ensuring that only the highest-quality beans make it to the next phase of production.

Drying the Beans

After cleaning, the beans are spread out under the sun to dry. This is a crucial step, as the beans must be dried to the perfect moisture level before they can be roasted. Farmers will often turn the beans throughout the drying process to ensure they dry evenly. The drying process can take several days, depending on the weather conditions, and it is essential that it is done slowly and carefully to preserve the integrity of the beans.

The sun-drying method used for Kopi Luwak helps maintain the natural flavors, and the slow process ensures that the beans retain their unique characteristics that will later shine through in the coffee cup.

Hulling and Sorting

Once dried, the beans are hulled to remove the parchment layer, revealing the green coffee beans inside. At this stage, the beans are carefully sorted by size, color, and overall quality. Sorting is done manually or using machines, ensuring that only the best beans continue through the process.

Farmers pay special attention during this phase to ensure that the beans are uniform in size, which will contribute to an even roast. The quality of the beans is critical in the production of Kopi Luwak, and each step is carefully monitored to ensure that only the finest beans are selected for roasting.

Roasting: The Art of Transformation

Roasting is a crucial step in the production of Kopi Luwak, as it unlocks the beans' full flavor potential. Roasting transforms the raw, green beans into the rich, aromatic coffee that so many people enjoy. Unlike mass-produced coffee, Kopi Luwak requires a more artisanal approach to roasting.

Expert roasters use precise techniques to highlight the natural sweetness and aroma of the beans while avoiding over-roasting, which could overshadow the delicate flavors. The roasting process is done in small batches to ensure consistency, and temperatures are carefully monitored to preserve the unique characteristics of the beans.

Roasting typically takes place at lower temperatures compared to other coffees, allowing for a slower and more even roast. The result is a coffee that is rich and smooth, with a slight caramelization of sugars that brings out the beans' natural flavors, from earthy notes to sweet, chocolatey undertones.

Grinding and Brewing

After roasting, the beans are ground to a desired consistency, depending on the brewing method being used. For an espresso, the grind may be fine, while for a French press, it would be coarser. The grind size is important because it affects the extraction of flavors during brewing.

When brewing, the method chosen plays a significant role in how the coffee's unique characteristics are showcased. Traditional methods like pour-over or French press allow for a more delicate extraction, bringing out the complex flavors of

Kopi Luwak. In contrast, espresso machines may concentrate the coffee's intense flavors in a smaller, richer serving.

Regardless of the brewing method, the goal is to extract the full potential of the beans while preserving their smoothness and the subtle fruity sweetness derived from the civet's selection process. Brewing methods like the Indonesian kopi tubruk (coffee brewed with sugar and boiled) also highlight its cultural significance.

Savoring the Experience

A cup of Kopi Luwak is much more than just a caffeine fix; it is a sensory journey. The rich aroma greets the drinker, followed by the smooth, velvety mouthfeel that only Kopi Luwak can deliver. The taste is complex yet balanced, with earthy undertones, a slight fruitiness, and a natural sweetness that lingers on the palate.

The coffee's low acidity makes it less harsh than regular coffee, and its richness makes each sip a meditative experience. Coffee enthusiasts savor the way the flavors evolve on the tongue, a testament to the natural fermentation process and the careful steps taken throughout its production.

The Environmental Impact of Kopi Luwak Production

While Kopi Luwak is a marvel of nature and craftsmanship, its production also raises important environmental and ethical concerns. The demand for this rare coffee has led to both positive and negative impacts on the ecosystems where civets live. In some regions, civets are kept in captivity to increase production, which has sparked debates over animal welfare and sustainable practices.

To mitigate these issues, there is a growing movement toward ethical, sustainable coffee farming, where civets are allowed to roam freely in the wild. This ensures that the coffee is not only produced in a humane manner but also preserves the delicate balance of the forest ecosystems that civets depend on.

Global Demand and Pricing of Kopi Luwak

The increasing global demand for Kopi Luwak has contributed to its status as one of the most expensive coffees in the world, with prices often reaching up to $1,000 per kilogram. This high cost is a result of the labor-intensive production process and the limited supply of wild civets.

However, the premium price tag has also led to the proliferation of counterfeit Kopi Luwak, and consumers are often faced with the challenge of distinguishing authentic beans from fake ones. Transparency in sourcing and production is key for consumers to ensure they are purchasing genuine Kopi Luwak that adheres to ethical standards.

Where to Find Kopi Luwak Around the World

Kopi Luwak has transcended its origins in Southeast Asia and is now available in gourmet cafes and high-end coffee shops worldwide. While it is still most commonly found in Indonesia, countries like the United States, Japan, and European nations have embraced its rarity and exceptional flavor.

To avoid purchasing substandard or unethical Kopi Luwak, it is essential for consumers to seek reputable sellers who ensure the humane treatment of civets and sustainable harvesting practices.

—

Chapter 3: The Modern Kopi Luwak Industry – From Tradition to Luxury

The history of Kopi Luwak spans centuries, and in recent decades, the coffee has become synonymous with luxury and exclusivity. This chapter explores how Kopi Luwak, once a local treasure, has evolved into one of the most coveted and expensive coffees in the world, delving into the industry's growth, marketing strategies, and challenges.

The Rise of Kopi Luwak's Popularity

In the 1990s, as global interest in specialty coffees grew, Kopi Luwak emerged as a niche product, intriguing coffee enthusiasts and travelers alike. Its exotic origin and the involvement of the civet made it stand out in the crowded coffee market. Word of mouth and media exposure further fueled its rise in popularity.

Initially, the production of Kopi Luwak remained relatively small-scale, with coffee farmers harvesting beans from wild civets. However, as demand soared, large-scale production methods emerged. Civets were kept in captivity on farms to produce higher quantities of beans, although this practice has been controversial due to concerns over animal welfare.

The Premium Price – What Makes Kopi Luwak So Expensive?

Several factors contribute to the high price of Kopi Luwak. First and foremost, the labor-intensive production process significantly increases costs. From the collection of the cherries to the meticulous cleaning, drying, and roasting processes, each step demands careful attention and expertise. The limited supply of wild civets also plays a significant role, as the beans they produce are rare and difficult to harvest.

Kopi Luwak's price also reflects its status as a luxury item. As demand grows, so does the prestige of owning and drinking this rare coffee. The unique story behind each cup, from the civet's digestive journey to the final brew, adds to the allure of the product.

Ethical Concerns and the Call for Sustainable Practices

As the popularity of Kopi Luwak increased, so did the ethical concerns surrounding its production. The practice of farming civets for coffee production has led to accusations of animal cruelty. In many farms, civets are kept in small cages, deprived of their natural habitat and forced to consume large quantities of coffee cherries.

To address these concerns, some companies and organizations have moved toward more ethical practices. Ethical farms allow civets to roam freely in the wild, ensuring they select the best cherries naturally, as they would in their natural environment. These farms also promote conservation efforts and fair trade principles, supporting both local communities and the ecosystems in which the civets live.

Consumers are increasingly aware of these issues, and many are choosing to support businesses that emphasize sustainability and animal welfare. Certification programs, such as those that ensure humane treatment of animals, have emerged as a way for consumers to distinguish between ethically produced Kopi Luwak and those that exploit animals.

Marketing Strategies and Global Availability

Kopi Luwak's marketing has been key to its success in the global coffee market. From the moment it became recognized as a luxury item, it was marketed as an exclusive experience. High-end coffee shops, luxury hotels, and specialty retailers began offering Kopi Luwak to their discerning customers, contributing to the coffee's premium image.

In addition to its status as a luxury commodity, Kopi Luwak is also marketed as an exotic experience. Its unique production process and the fascinating journey of the beans through the civet's digestive system are emphasized in marketing materials to attract coffee aficionados and curious consumers.

Today, Kopi Luwak can be found in upscale coffee shops and gourmet retailers across the globe. While its origins remain tied to Southeast Asia, the coffee has become a symbol of exclusivity in cities like New York, London, Tokyo, and Paris. However, finding authentic Kopi Luwak requires careful sourcing, as counterfeit or misrepresented products have flooded the market.

Where to Find Kopi Luwak Around the World

Though the heart of Kopi Luwak's production remains in Southeast Asia, specifically Indonesia, Vietnam, and the Philippines, its global presence has expanded rapidly. Today, coffee lovers from all corners of the world can savor a cup of this rare brew.

In Indonesia, particularly in Bali and Sumatra, Kopi Luwak is sold at coffee plantations, where tourists can learn about the production process firsthand. The coffee is also widely available in high-end cafes in major cities, including Jakarta, Singapore, and Kuala Lumpur. For international customers, online retailers offer Kopi Luwak, often with detailed information about the sourcing and production methods to ensure authenticity.

Despite its widespread availability, authenticity remains a concern. Consumers are urged to buy Kopi Luwak from reputable sources that guarantee ethical practices and high-quality beans. Genuine Kopi Luwak is typically sold in small batches, and a premium price is expected for authentic, high-quality beans.

The Challenges of Counterfeiting and Misrepresentation

As the demand for Kopi Luwak has grown, so has the risk of counterfeiting and fraud. Unscrupulous sellers have flooded the market with fake Kopi Luwak, using beans from non-wild civets or even beans from different coffee species altogether. These counterfeit products often fail to live up to the unique flavor profile of true Kopi Luwak and contribute to the misleading portrayal of the coffee in the marketplace.

To combat this issue, certification programs and third-party verifications have become more common in the Kopi Luwak industry. Consumers can now check for certifications that guarantee the coffee's authenticity, ensuring they are purchasing a product that adheres to ethical and quality standards.

The Future of Kopi Luwak

Looking ahead, the future of Kopi Luwak is shaped by two key factors: sustainability and innovation. As the demand for rare and specialty coffees continues to rise, producers must find a balance between maintaining the quality and exclusivity of Kopi Luwak while addressing ethical concerns and environmental impact.

New methods of production, including the development of sustainable farming practices and animal welfare certifications, will likely play a crucial role in the future of the industry. With increasing awareness of the importance of ethical practices, the coffee world is evolving to prioritize not only exceptional flavor but also the well-being of the creatures that make this coffee possible.

At the same time, the desire for unique, high-quality coffee will continue to drive interest in Kopi Luwak. As consumers seek out new and exciting coffee experiences, the legacy of Kopi Luwak, rooted in tradition yet evolving with the times, will likely remain a symbol of luxury, rarity, and taste.

Conclusion

Kopi Luwak, with its remarkable journey from the civet's digestive tract to the coffee cup, represents both a piece of Southeast Asian history and a modern luxury item. As the coffee industry moves toward more sustainable practices and greater transparency, the future of Kopi Luwak remains as intriguing as its past.

This chapter explored the growth of Kopi Luwak from a traditional, local product to a global symbol of exclusivity and luxury. The challenges surrounding its ethical production and marketing strategies reveal the complex interplay of tradition, sustainability, and demand in the coffee world. With careful attention to the preservation of both the civet population and the natural environment, Kopi Luwak has the potential to continue captivating coffee enthusiasts for generations to come.

—

Chapter 4: Ethical Sourcing and Sustainability in Kopi Luwak Production

As the popularity of Kopi Luwak grows, so does the concern over its ethical and sustainable production. While the traditional method of harvesting Kopi Luwak is a unique and fascinating process, it has also raised significant ethical questions about the welfare of the civets involved. This chapter explores the key ethical issues surrounding the production of Kopi Luwak, as well as the growing movement toward sustainable farming practices.

The Ethical Dilemma of Captive Civets

The most contentious issue surrounding Kopi Luwak production is the treatment of civets in captivity. In many cases, civets are kept in small cages, where they are often deprived of their natural environment and forced to consume large quantities of coffee cherries. These conditions have led to widespread criticism from animal rights organizations, as the civets' natural behaviors are restricted, and they may suffer from poor health and malnutrition.

In addition to the physical harm caused by confinement, there are concerns about the psychological stress experienced by civets in captivity. Civets are solitary animals by nature, and being kept in overcrowded cages can lead to stress, anxiety, and behavioral problems.

The Impact on Wild Civet Populations

Another significant concern is the impact of Kopi Luwak production on wild civet populations. As demand for the coffee increases, some producers resort to trapping wild civets to meet the supply. This practice poses a threat to the natural populations of civets, many of which are already facing habitat loss due to deforestation and human encroachment.

The decline in wild civet populations not only threatens biodiversity but also undermines the authenticity of Kopi Luwak. As the availability of wild civet beans decreases, the practice of farming civets in captivity has become more widespread, further distancing the coffee from its traditional, natural origins.

The Rise of Ethical and Sustainable Kopi Luwak

In response to these ethical concerns, many producers are shifting toward more sustainable and humane methods of producing Kopi Luwak. The movement for ethical Kopi Luwak production emphasizes two key principles: humane treatment of animals and the preservation of natural habitats.

Free-Range Civet Farming

One of the most important innovations in sustainable Kopi Luwak production is the practice of free-range civet farming. Unlike traditional farms where civets are kept in cages, free-range farms allow civets to roam freely in the wild or in semi-wild environments. On these farms, civets can forage for coffee cherries naturally, just as they would in their native habitats, ensuring that they are not subjected to the stress and confinement of captivity.

Free-range civet farming also promotes biodiversity and environmental sustainability. By allowing civets to interact with their natural surroundings, these farms help preserve the ecosystems that support both the civets and the coffee plants. The beans harvested from free-range civets are often considered superior in quality, as the civets are able to select the best cherries and contribute to the complex flavor profile that defines high-quality Kopi Luwak.

Fair-Trade and Community-Based Initiatives

Many ethical Kopi Luwak producers are also embracing fair trade principles, ensuring that farmers and local communities receive fair compensation for their work. These initiatives aim to empower local coffee growers by providing them with better access to markets and promoting sustainable agricultural practices. By supporting small-scale farmers, these initiatives help reduce the environmental impact of large-scale coffee production and foster a sense of community involvement.

Fair-trade certifications often include guidelines on environmental stewardship, which encourage farmers to use organic farming methods and avoid harmful pesticides and chemicals. These practices not only improve the quality of the coffee but also help preserve the soil and water resources that are essential for sustainable coffee farming.

The Role of Certification Programs

Certification programs, such as the Rainforest Alliance and Organic certification, have become increasingly important in the Kopi Luwak industry. These programs provide third-party verification that the coffee has been produced in accordance with strict environmental and social standards. For consumers, these certifications offer reassurance that the coffee they are purchasing has been sourced ethically and sustainably.

For producers, obtaining certification can open up new markets and opportunities for growth. Consumers are increasingly aware of the ethical and environmental implications of their purchases, and many are willing to pay a premium for products that are certified as sustainable and humane.

Educating Consumers About Ethical Kopi Luwak

One of the challenges facing the Kopi Luwak industry is educating consumers about the ethical implications of their choices. While many coffee enthusiasts are drawn to the unique taste and story behind Kopi Luwak, few are aware of the ethical issues associated with its production. As the demand for ethical products grows, it is essential for producers to educate consumers about the importance of choosing sustainably sourced Kopi Luwak.

Increased awareness can lead to a shift in consumer behavior, with more people opting for ethically sourced Kopi Luwak. This, in turn, can incentivize producers to adopt more humane practices and help create a more sustainable future for the coffee industry.

Challenges in Transitioning to Ethical Practices

Despite the growing movement toward ethical Kopi Luwak, transitioning from traditional farming methods to more sustainable practices is not without its challenges. Free-range civet farming, for example, requires significant investment in land, infrastructure, and knowledge of animal behavior. Moreover, the limited availability of wild civets makes it difficult to meet the growing demand for Kopi Luwak without resorting to farming civets in captivity.

Additionally, the premium price of ethically sourced Kopi Luwak can be a barrier for some consumers. While the ethical and environmental benefits are clear, the higher cost of production is reflected in the price of the coffee. This makes it difficult for some consumers to afford the coffee, limiting its market appeal.

The Future of Ethical Kopi Luwak

Looking to the future, the success of ethical Kopi Luwak production will depend on continued innovation and collaboration across the coffee industry. By working together, farmers, producers, and consumers can help ensure that Kopi Luwak is produced in a way that is both sustainable and humane. With the right support, the Kopi Luwak industry has the potential to thrive in a way that respects both the animals and the environment, while still delivering the exceptional taste and quality that coffee lovers around the world have come to expect.

As consumer demand for ethically produced coffee grows, so too will the pressure on producers to meet higher standards of sustainability and animal welfare. The future of Kopi Luwak is in the hands of those who care about the story behind the beans, the welfare of the civets, and the long-term sustainability of the coffee industry.

Conclusion

The journey of Kopi Luwak, from a unique and exotic coffee to a luxury product enjoyed worldwide, has been marked by both fascination and controversy. As the coffee industry evolves, ethical sourcing and sustainability will play an increasingly important role in shaping the future of Kopi Luwak production. By embracing free-range civet farming, fair trade practices, and certification programs, the Kopi Luwak industry can help ensure that this remarkable coffee continues to be enjoyed by future generations while respecting the animals and ecosystems that make it possible.

—

Chapter 5: The Global Market for Kopi Luwak: Price, Popularity, and Accessibility

Kopi Luwak, once a local delicacy in the Indonesian archipelago, has gained international recognition and become a symbol of luxury and rarity in the global coffee market. However, this rise to fame has not come without its challenges. In this chapter, we explore how Kopi Luwak has found its place in the global marketplace, the factors contributing to its high price, and the places where you can find this coveted coffee today.

From Local Treasure to Global Luxury

Kopi Luwak's journey from a traditional drink to a luxury item has been both fascinating and complex. The coffee's origins in Southeast Asia, particularly in Indonesia, were rooted in local traditions where indigenous farmers discovered that civets, or "luwak," consumed the best coffee cherries and later excreted them. The beans, after being collected, cleaned, and processed, were found to have unique flavor characteristics, which quickly became prized among coffee aficionados.

While initially a product enjoyed by small local communities, the recognition of Kopi Luwak's unique processing method and rich flavor soon spread to coffee enthusiasts around the world. As international demand grew, so did the price of Kopi Luwak. It became regarded as one of the most expensive coffees in the world, fetching prices that can range from $100 to $600 per pound, depending on its grade and production method.

Factors Contributing to High Prices

Several factors contribute to the high price tag associated with Kopi Luwak. First and foremost, the labor-intensive production process plays a significant role. Unlike traditional coffee beans that are harvested by hand from coffee plants, Kopi Luwak requires the involvement of civets, whose digestion process imparts a unique flavor profile to the beans. This means that every batch of Kopi Luwak requires careful collection, cleaning, and sorting of beans that have been ingested by civets.

The scarcity of wild civets and the limited supply of high-quality beans also add to the cost. In recent years, demand for Kopi Luwak has outpaced its supply, leading to increased prices. Additionally, ethical production practices, such as free-range civet farming and organic certification, often result in higher production costs, which are reflected in the price of the coffee.

Another factor driving up the price is the exclusivity associated with Kopi Luwak. Due to the limited nature of the coffee and its labor-intensive production, it is often marketed as a luxury item. As with many luxury goods, exclusivity adds to its appeal, and coffee drinkers are willing to pay a premium for the status of consuming a rare and expensive product.

The Global Popularity of Kopi Luwak

As demand for high-quality coffee continues to rise, Kopi Luwak has carved out a niche in the global coffee market. Its reputation for being an exotic, luxury coffee has made it particularly popular among coffee connoisseurs, celebrities, and high-end restaurants and hotels. The allure of Kopi Luwak is not just about its unique production process but also the experience of drinking a cup of coffee with a distinct story behind it.

The growing popularity of specialty coffee worldwide has also contributed to the rise of Kopi Luwak. In many parts of the world, coffee lovers are increasingly seeking out premium, rare, and sustainably sourced coffee beans. For these consumers, Kopi Luwak represents the pinnacle of coffee culture – a rare, indulgent experience that goes beyond the typical cup of coffee.

Countries such as the United States, Japan, China, and the United Arab Emirates have become key markets for Kopi Luwak. In these regions, high-end cafes and restaurants have embraced the coffee, offering it as part of their exclusive menus. Additionally, online retailers and specialty coffee shops have made it easier than ever for consumers to purchase Kopi Luwak and have it delivered to their doorsteps, further expanding its reach.

Where in the World Can You Find Kopi Luwak?

Despite its growing popularity, Kopi Luwak remains a niche product that is not widely available in every coffee shop or supermarket. However, as demand continues to rise, it has become more accessible to coffee drinkers around the world. Here are some of the key regions where you can find this luxurious coffee:

Southeast Asia: The Heart of Kopi Luwak

Indonesia remains the birthplace of Kopi Luwak and continues to be its primary source. In Indonesia, particularly on the islands of Java, Sumatra, and Bali, Kopi Luwak is often sold at local cafes and small boutique coffee shops. Many coffee plantations in the region offer tourists the opportunity to visit their farms, observe the coffee production process, and taste freshly brewed Kopi Luwak on-site.

In other Southeast Asian countries, such as the Philippines, Thailand, and Vietnam, Kopi Luwak has also gained popularity. Although the production of Kopi Luwak in these countries is not as widespread as in Indonesia, it is still possible to find specialty coffee shops that offer the coffee to discerning customers.

The United States and Europe: Coffee Culture at Its Best

In the United States and Europe, Kopi Luwak has found a home in upscale cafes and specialty coffee shops. These regions are home to coffee lovers who appreciate the artistry and rarity of high-end coffee. Many luxury hotels and five-star restaurants in cities such as New York, Paris, London, and Milan offer Kopi Luwak as part of their premium coffee offerings.

In the United States, online platforms such as Amazon and specialty coffee retailers also provide access to Kopi Luwak, making it easier for consumers across the country to try the coffee. While the price remains a barrier for many, the growing interest in specialty coffee has led to an increase in availability in cafes and restaurants catering to high-end clientele.

The Middle East and Asia: Luxury Markets and Affluent Consumers

In the Middle East, particularly in the United Arab Emirates, Kopi Luwak has become a symbol of luxury and exclusivity. High-end cafes, five-star hotels, and upscale restaurants in cities like Dubai and Abu Dhabi offer Kopi Luwak as part of their exclusive menus. The demand for rare and prestigious products is particularly high in this region, where coffee culture has become a blend of tradition and luxury.

Similarly, countries like Japan and China, where coffee culture has been growing in recent years, have also seen an increase in the demand for Kopi Luwak. In Japan, the coffee is often sold in premium coffee shops, and in China, where coffee drinking is becoming more popular among affluent consumers, Kopi Luwak is often seen as a status symbol.

The Future of Kopi Luwak in the Global Market

As the global coffee market continues to expand and diversify, the future of Kopi Luwak remains promising. While the high price and limited availability may make it a niche product, its allure as a luxury item and its unique production process ensure that it will continue to capture the attention of coffee lovers worldwide.

However, as the demand for Kopi Luwak grows, it is crucial that the industry addresses the ethical concerns surrounding its production. By supporting sustainable farming practices, ethical sourcing, and fair trade initiatives, the Kopi Luwak industry can ensure that this beloved coffee remains both a luxury and a force for good in the global market.

Conclusion

Kopi Luwak has transformed from a local curiosity to one of the most sought-after luxury coffee products in the world. Its rise to fame has been driven by its unique production method, scarcity, and association with exclusivity. As demand for the coffee grows, it is becoming more accessible to coffee drinkers around the world. However, it is essential that the Kopi Luwak industry prioritizes sustainability and ethical practices to ensure that the coffee remains a force for good while continuing to deliver the exceptional taste that has made it famous.

—

Chapter 6: The Health Benefits and Stomach-Friendly Properties of Kopi Luwak

Coffee has long been celebrated for its energizing effects, but not all coffee is created equal. Among the many varieties of coffee beans, Kopi Luwak stands out not only for its unique production process but also for the potential health benefits it offers. In this chapter, we delve into the health aspects of Kopi Luwak, focusing particularly on its effects on the stomach and digestion, as well as its other potential health advantages.

Why Kopi Luwak May Be Gentler on Your Stomach

For many people, coffee can be hard on the stomach. The acidity in traditional coffee can lead to discomfort, including acid reflux, heartburn, and stomach irritation. Kopi Luwak, however, is often considered a gentler alternative for those who experience these issues with regular coffee.

The primary reason Kopi Luwak is often easier on the stomach lies in its unique fermentation process. After the civet consumes the coffee cherries, the beans undergo a fermentation process in the digestive tract, which can reduce the acidity of the beans. This fermentation process is thought to break down certain compounds in the beans that contribute to their bitterness and acidity. As a result, Kopi Luwak is often described as having a smoother, milder taste compared to regular coffee, with less of the sharp, acidic bite that can irritate sensitive stomachs.

Moreover, the beans that pass through the civet's digestive system are also partially cleaned during the process, which can result in a coffee that is free from some of the common irritants found in conventionally processed beans. This makes it an appealing option for those who are sensitive to the acidity and harshness of regular coffee.

Kopi Luwak and Digestive Health

In addition to being gentler on the stomach, some studies suggest that Kopi Luwak may have beneficial effects on digestion due to its lower acidity and the presence of specific enzymes that are believed to be retained during the fermentation process. These enzymes may help support the breakdown of food in the stomach, potentially promoting better digestion and reducing bloating.

While the health benefits of Kopi Luwak in terms of digestion are not yet fully understood, it is clear that its smoother, less acidic profile can make it a more suitable choice for people who experience digestive discomfort from drinking regular coffee. This could be especially beneficial for individuals who suffer from conditions like gastritis, ulcers, or acid reflux.

The Antioxidant Content of Kopi Luwak

Like all coffee, Kopi Luwak is rich in antioxidants, compounds that are known for their ability to neutralize harmful free radicals in the body. Free radicals can contribute to aging, inflammation, and various chronic diseases, including heart disease and cancer. Antioxidants, therefore, play a crucial role in promoting overall health and well-being.

Kopi Luwak contains a variety of antioxidants, including polyphenols, which are known for their anti-inflammatory properties. These antioxidants can help protect cells from oxidative stress and reduce the risk of chronic diseases. Additionally, antioxidants are believed to support immune function, reduce inflammation, and improve skin health by fighting the effects of aging.

While the antioxidant content in Kopi Luwak may vary depending on the specific batch and production process, it is generally considered to be on par with other high-quality coffee varieties. For those seeking to enjoy the health benefits of coffee, Kopi Luwak offers a premium option that combines both flavor and potential health advantages.

Kopi Luwak and Caffeine Content

One of the most well-known benefits of coffee is its caffeine content, which is known for its ability to boost energy and improve mental alertness. However, for some people, the caffeine in regular coffee can cause jitteriness, anxiety, or digestive issues. Kopi Luwak, however, contains slightly less caffeine than traditional coffee beans, making it a better option for those who are sensitive to caffeine.

The reduced caffeine content may be a result of the fermentation process that occurs in the civet's digestive system. While the exact amount of caffeine in Kopi Luwak can vary, many consumers report that they experience a smoother, more sustained energy boost without the nervousness or stomach upset that sometimes accompanies regular coffee.

For individuals looking to enjoy the stimulating effects of coffee without overloading on caffeine, Kopi Luwak offers a more moderate option that still delivers a rich and satisfying cup of coffee.

Potential Risks of Kopi Luwak

While Kopi Luwak offers several potential health benefits, it is important to note that there are a few considerations to keep in mind when consuming this luxury coffee. As with any coffee, drinking it in excess can lead to negative side effects, including increased heart rate, insomnia, and digestive disturbances.

Furthermore, some ethical concerns have arisen in recent years regarding the production of Kopi Luwak. In some cases, civets are kept in captivity and forced to eat coffee cherries in an inhumane manner. This not only raises animal welfare issues but can also lead to lower-quality coffee and potential health risks from improper processing. It is essential to ensure that any Kopi Luwak you purchase is sourced ethically, with civets being treated with care and respect.

Additionally, because Kopi Luwak is a premium product, it can be quite expensive. As with any luxury item, it is important to be cautious of counterfeit or low-quality Kopi Luwak that may not deliver the same health benefits as authentic, ethically produced coffee.

Conclusion

Kopi Luwak is not only a luxury coffee with a rich and unique flavor profile, but it also offers a range of potential health benefits. Its lower acidity and smoother taste make it a more stomach-friendly option for those who experience discomfort from regular coffee. The antioxidant content and moderate caffeine levels further enhance its appeal as a health-conscious choice for coffee lovers.

However, as with all foods and beverages, it is important to enjoy Kopi Luwak in moderation and to choose ethically sourced, high-quality beans to ensure you are benefiting from the coffee's health advantages while avoiding potential risks.

—

Chapter 7: A Comparison of Kopi Luwak and Other Coffee Varieties

Kopi Luwak, known for its unique production process and luxurious reputation, stands out in the world of coffee. But how does it compare to other types of coffee? In this chapter, we will explore the key differences between Kopi Luwak and other popular coffee varieties, such as Arabica and Robusta. By examining factors such as taste, price, production methods, and global demand, we can better understand why Kopi Luwak commands such a premium price and how it fits into the broader coffee landscape.

Taste and Flavor Profile

One of the most significant distinctions between Kopi Luwak and other coffee beans is its flavor profile. The beans undergo a unique fermentation process inside the civet's digestive system, which alters their chemical composition and ultimately affects the taste. Kopi Luwak is known for its smooth, less acidic taste, with notes that can include earthy, chocolatey, or fruity flavors, depending on the region and beans used.

Arabica:

Arabica coffee beans are widely regarded for their sweet, mild flavor, often described as having fruity, floral, or nutty notes. Arabica beans tend to have a higher acidity compared to Kopi Luwak, which gives them a sharper taste. The flavor is often more complex, with distinct fruity and berry-like undertones.

Robusta:

Robusta coffee beans are known for their stronger, more robust flavor, often described as bitter, earthy, and somewhat harsh. They tend to have a higher caffeine content than Arabica beans and a thicker crema. Robusta coffee is generally less refined and has a more astringent taste compared to the smoothness of Kopi Luwak.

Kopi Luwak's lower acidity and more rounded flavor profile make it an appealing choice for those who are sensitive to the bitterness and sharpness found in other coffee varieties, such as Robusta and some Arabicas.

Production Process

The production process is where Kopi Luwak truly differentiates itself from other coffees. While Arabica and Robusta are harvested from coffee trees and undergo a relatively standard process of drying, roasting, and grinding, Kopi Luwak takes a much more unusual route.

Kopi Luwak:

The beans of Kopi Luwak are first eaten by civet cats, which then pass them through their digestive system. The beans are collected from the feces of the civet, cleaned, and processed. The fermentation process that occurs within the civet's stomach is believed to remove some of the bitterness and acidity from the beans, resulting in a smoother cup of coffee.

Arabica and Robusta:

Both Arabica and Robusta beans are grown on coffee plantations, where they are handpicked or harvested by machines. The beans are then washed, dried, and roasted in traditional ways. Unlike Kopi Luwak, there is no digestive fermentation process involved in the production of Arabica and Robusta beans, which can contribute to their higher acidity and distinct flavor profiles.

The labor-intensive process of producing Kopi Luwak, along with its unique fermentation method, contributes to the coffee's rarity and high price. In contrast, Arabica and Robusta are grown in large quantities around the world, making them more affordable and widely available.

Price and Rarity

Kopi Luwak is widely regarded as one of the most expensive coffees in the world. The rarity of the coffee, due to the labor-intensive process and the fact that only small amounts of beans are produced each year, makes it a luxury item. Authentic, high-quality Kopi Luwak can cost hundreds of dollars per kilogram, with a cup of coffee often priced at $30 or more.

Arabica:

Arabica beans are considered premium beans and typically cost more than Robusta beans. However, they are still far more affordable than Kopi Luwak, with prices ranging from $15 to $30 per kilogram, depending on the region and quality. Arabica coffee is also the most popular coffee variety worldwide, making it much more widely available.

Robusta:

Robusta coffee is the most common and least expensive variety of coffee. It is often used in mass-market coffee blends, particularly for espresso. Due to its widespread availability and lower production costs, Robusta beans are much more affordable, typically priced at $5 to $10 per kilogram.

The rarity and labor-intensive production process of Kopi Luwak make it significantly more expensive than both Arabica and Robusta, making it a luxury product enjoyed by coffee connoisseurs around the world.

Global Demand and Popularity

Kopi Luwak, due to its exclusivity and association with luxury, has seen a growing demand, particularly in high-end coffee markets and among coffee aficionados. Its reputation as a rare, exotic product has led to increased interest in the coffee, though the ethical concerns surrounding its production have led some consumers to be more cautious in their purchasing decisions.

Arabica:

Arabica coffee, being the most widely consumed coffee in the world, has a massive global demand. It is grown in regions such as Central and South America, Africa, and parts of Asia, and is consumed by millions of people every day. Arabica coffee is often seen as the "standard" coffee, and its versatility makes it suitable for a wide range of brewing methods, from espresso to drip coffee.

Robusta:

Robusta coffee is particularly popular in Europe and parts of Asia, especially in espresso blends and instant coffee. While it has a smaller share of the global coffee market compared to Arabica, it is still widely consumed due to its affordability and strong flavor.

Kopi Luwak's demand remains more niche compared to Arabica and Robusta, though it continues to attract a loyal following of coffee lovers who are willing to pay a premium for its unique flavor and production process.

Ethical Considerations

As Kopi Luwak gains in popularity, there have been increasing concerns over the ethical treatment of the civets involved in the coffee's production. In some cases, civets are kept in captivity and force-fed coffee cherries, leading to questions about animal welfare and the sustainability of the coffee's production.

Arabica and Robusta:

While ethical concerns about farming practices and labor conditions exist for all types of coffee, Arabica and Robusta are generally produced in more conventional ways, with less controversy over the treatment of animals. That said, both types of coffee are still subject to issues such as fair trade practices, deforestation, and sustainability in coffee-growing regions.

Consumers who are concerned about the ethical implications of their coffee purchases should seek out Kopi Luwak that is sourced from responsible producers who prioritize animal welfare and environmentally sustainable practices.

Conclusion

While Kopi Luwak stands out for its distinctive production process, unique flavor, and high price, it is just one among many varieties of coffee. Each coffee type—whether it's the mild and sweet Arabica, the strong and bitter Robusta, or the luxurious

Kopi Luwak—offers something different for the discerning coffee lover.

Kopi Luwak's smoothness and reduced acidity make it an attractive choice for those seeking a more refined coffee experience, but its rarity and ethical considerations also set it apart from more widely available options. Whether you are a connoisseur or a casual coffee drinker, understanding the differences between these coffee varieties can help you make an informed decision the next time you pick up a cup.

—

Conclusion

Kopi Luwak has captivated the world with its extraordinary production process, smooth flavor, and exclusive reputation. From its origins in Southeast Asia to its rise as one of the most expensive and sought-after coffee varieties, the journey of Kopi Luwak is nothing short of fascinating. However, as we've explored in this book, its story is not just about the unique method of fermentation or its price tag. It's also about the ethical considerations, sustainability, and respect for the animals involved in its production. With this knowledge, consumers can enjoy Kopi Luwak with a deeper appreciation for the complexity of the coffee and the responsibilities that come with it.

While Kopi Luwak may remain a luxurious treat for some, it has undeniably earned its place in the global coffee landscape. Whether it is the smoothness, the rarity, or the story behind every cup, Kopi Luwak offers a unique coffee experience like no other.

—

Acknowledgments

First and foremost, I would like to express my deepest gratitude to all the dedicated farmers, civet caretakers, and coffee artisans who make the production of Kopi Luwak possible. Your hard work, passion, and commitment to your craft are what bring this exceptional coffee to the world.

I would also like to thank the readers for taking the time to explore the story of Kopi Luwak with me. Whether you are a coffee enthusiast, a curious traveler, or someone looking to understand more about the world's most expensive coffee, your interest in this subject helps keep the conversation about coffee culture alive.

Lastly, I would like to thank my family and friends for their unwavering support throughout the writing process. Your encouragement and belief in me have been invaluable.

Don't miss out!

Visit the website below and you can sign up to receive emails whenever Dans Hardyans publishes a new book. There's no charge and no obligation.

https://books2read.com/r/B-A-ULFBD-BRRLF

BOOKS 2 READ

Connecting independent readers to independent writers.

Also by Dans Hardyans

The Kopi Luwak Legacy: Tradition, Taste and Truth
Unveiling The Veil Two Nation: Israel and Palestine